Coaching the Quarterback Mesh

A Complete System for Coaching Quarterbacks to Run Any Option Play

Table of Contents

Teaching the Mesh in Stages

The Mesh is the hardest skill in football to develop. It combines precise footwork with split second decision making. The pressure of making a correct decision in the mesh is a difficult position to put any Quarterback in which is why it is so crucial to develop a system for teaching and drilling the techniques necessary to make a correct read. Once this system has been developed it's important that it is repped on an everyday basis. The Quarterback must be able to react on instincts to make the instantaneous decisions that are required when reading the mesh.

In order to teach the Mesh successfully the Quarterback's role should be broken down into 4 stages: Pre-Snap, Pre-Mesh, Mid-Mesh and Post-Mesh. In any option play these stages must be completed in order to have a successful mesh. For offenses as different as Georgia Tech's Flexbone Ball Control Spread Option Attack to Oregon's Ultra High Tempo Air Raid Based Spread Option many of these mechanics remain the same for the Quarterback.

The Stages

1. Pre-Snap: Setting the Table

2. Pre-Mesh Position: Position and Preparation

3. Mid Mesh: Engage and Decide

4. Post Mesh: Disengage and Accelerate

5. Pitch/Pass: Feed the Speed

Pre-Snap: Set the Table

One of the most important parts of any read play is the Quarterbacks Pre-Snap progression and reads. The first thing the QB has to do before the ball is snapped is identify the Read Man. This will be the player he will read to determine if he is giving or keeping the ball. Obviously the player he will be reading can vary from play to play. The QB also needs to identify that player's assignment in the structure of the defense before the snap of the ball. Sometimes this can be very easy to tell, other times it can be difficult. One of the best ways to understand a defenders responsibility is to look at the players around him and remembering defenses must account for every gap on a run play.

While the QB is doing this it's important that he doesn't give hints to the defense on what the play the offense will be running. One way to prevent this is by having the QB go through the same process every time he comes to the line. This will make sure the defense can't ID which side the play is going to.

Another way to make sure the QB doesn't tip his hand this is to not call a direction for the play but instead make it a check at the line. It can be stressful to give the quarterback the power to audible at the Line of Scrimmage. To combat this the QB must have a very clear set of rules to follow in order to make an audible. This, combined with confidence and trust, will allow him to make a choice and put the offense in the best play against that defensive front.

Pre-Mesh Position: Position and Preparation

The footwork of how the QB arrives at the pre-mesh position for a given option play can vary greatly from play to play but each QB must get into a good Pre-Mesh Position in order for the read to be successful. The keys to a great Pre-Mesh Position are Ball Position, Eyes on Target and Athletic Position.

First the ball must be stretched back so the running back can run the ball through the mesh. (Note: There are varying schools of thought here. I am a believer in the ride method over the point method so I will just talk to that.) This should happen while the QB is getting his feet in their correct position. As the QB reaches the mesh he should snap the ball back as far as possible on a flat even plane.

By stretching the ball back as far as possible the QB gives himself a longer time to make the read. The longer the QB has the ball in the pocket the more time he has to make a choice. Because the QB has until the ball reaches his front hip to make a decision on the mesh he can only lengthen the read by stretching the ball back. In addition to this a long ride will make it harder for the defense to see who has the ball.

The second major point of the Pre-Mesh Position is that the eyes should be on the defender. We will get to reading the defender in the next phase but the QB must have his eyes on that defender immediately. We tell the QB and RB that the RB is responsible for running over the ball since the QB is in charge of making the defender wrong. This means the QB no longer has to worry about putting the ball into the RB's stomach, instead the QB stretches it back and the RB is responsible for his pocket onto the ball.

The last major point in the Pre-Mesh Position is that the QB must stay in an athletic position. One tactic some teams will use to defend the option is to charge the mesh, others will send a "Blood Stunt" where two defenders blitz directly off the edge. The QB must be in an athletic position so that if he does get a mesh charge, blood stunt or any thing that makes him worry, he can disconnect and make a play.

Mid-Mesh Position: Engage and Decide

Making the final choice on a mesh is one of the most difficult skills in football. It is a decision that must be made in a split second and can result in a negative play, a turnover or a touchdown. This makes it an important skill that must be practiced a million times over the course of a season.

Before addressing the decision making process it's important to talk about the body mechanics the QB will use throughout the mesh. The mesh starts when the ball hits the FB's belly. Once the ball hits the RBs belly the QB must enter into a position of shared possession with the RB. The QB wants to loosen his grip up so he has a firm but light hold on the ball. One thing that QBs tend to struggle with is that they want to carry the ball forward. The fix to this is to tell them they are like a loaded spring, once they set the ball back in their pre-mesh position it is only the RB's stomach and forward momentum that will push the ball forward.

As the ball comes forward the QB should be shifting his weight to match the ball. This means that in the pre-mesh position, where the ball is stretched back, all of the QBs weight should be on the back foot. As the ball continues forward his weight will move forward to match the placement of the ball. At the end of the mesh all of his weight should be on his front foot as the RB reaches the QBs front hip. When the RB reaches the front hip the QB must make his choice and either give the ball and carry out his fake or pull the ball and continue on to the next part of the play.

One way to make this choice easier is to give your QB a one way decision making process. This allows him to simplify the decision making process and make a quicker decision. In order to do this the instruction to the QB are that he is going to hand off the ball unless _____. There are a couple of options for what to put in that blank which are discussed below.

When teaching a QB to read a defender there are multiple ways to breakdown what the QB should be looking at. It's best to go over all of these options with the QB as each has it's own strengths and weaknesses. One of the more popular places to read is the near shoulder. In this read the QB will give the ball unless that near shoulder commits to the dive back.

Another, similar option, is the near hip, again it is a give unless the hip comes towards the dive key. One interesting way of making a read is to focus on the defenders eyes, if he isn't looking at the RB he can't tackle him. It can be pretty difficult to determine where the read player is looking but some QBs swear by it. Other options of focus points are far number or either knee.

There are a million different things QB's can read but it's important to not over coach the mesh. Once the QB starts to get a good feel for reading the mesh you can simplify things by telling him to give the ball unless the defender can tackle the ball carrier for less than 3 yards. By not over coaching it the QB gets a feel for how to read the intentions of defenders.

Post Mesh: Disengage and Accelerate

The disconnection is one of the most under coached parts of the mesh. The Quarterbacks actions once he disconnects from the mesh, whether he is moving on to another option, running the ball himself or carrying out a fake can make or break a play.

If he does hand off the ball to the RB he must accelerate off of his fake with his hands in the correct position. Many times a QB will carry out a half effort fake down the field but never have a change of speed. In reality the first three steps after a handoff are the most important. These are the three steps that will stop a read key from chasing down the RB or influence a second or third level player to chase the QB and get out of position which opens up a lane for the RB.

What sells any fake is acceleration off of the handoff and hand position that looks like the QB has the ball. Defenders can rarely see the ball when it is tucked away either in the 5 points of pressure position (running position) or in the cradle position (throwing/pitching position). By accelerating off the ball the QB makes it more difficult for the defender to get a good look at the ball and if his hands are in the correct spot they can't get a clear picture. This means must respect the threat of the QB which takes them out of the play.

If the QB does not get a handoff read he is now responsible for executing the next phase of his option. This requires him to accelerate off the mesh point. This acceleration is the reason why it is so important all of his weight loads onto his front foot at the end of the mesh. This allows his first step to be with his back leg. If the QB accelerates and steps with his front foot first he risks tripping up the RB.

If the QB is running with the ball he must tuck the ball into the 5 points of pressure position and get his eyes in the hole right away. It is important that he stay low and accelerate so that he can take advantage of the defenders who have committed to the dive back.

If the QB has a second option, whether it be throwing vs. running or pitching vs. running, the key is to get the eyes on the second read immediately. Many times defense will use Gap Exchange blitzes or blood stunts to give the QB a pull read and then blitz a defender directly to him. It's important the QB is ready for that so he is always prepared for a blood stunt when he disconnects. When drilling the second phase of the option it's important to give the QB a hurried blitz look more often than he will see it in the game so that he can prepare.

Pitch/Pass: Feed the Speed

After the mesh many option plays will include a second choice the Quarterback must make. He will have the option to either run the ball or pitch it to a pitch back. As offenses have evolved many times the Quarterback will have the option to throw the ball to a receiver downfield instead of pitching it. While these are different skills the thought process that the Quarterback goes through is very similar.

When the Quarterback does get a pitch/pass read he must deliver a ball that is accurate, catchable and puts his play in a position to make a big play in space. The worst thing that can happen is that the ball ends up in the defense's hands. For this reason the Quarterback will only pitch/pass the ball if he is 100% certain it will be caught. If he has any doubts he will keep the ball and live for the next play.

When reading the pitch key the QB is reading a player in space. This makes it a much more dynamic read because it is an open field read with lots of room which forces the quarterback to read the defender's body language. By attacking downhill the Quarterback limits the amount of feathering that the pitch key can do and forces him to declare his intentions. Feathering is when the pitch key does not commit to the QB or pitch man but tries to string the play out. When the QB attacks downhill and gets a feather technique it is very easy for him to plant give a quick fake pitch and get up field.

When pitching the ball there are a variety of different ways to pitch it but pitching the ball by tuning the thumb down is the most the most universal way to execute the pitch. The main coaching point with the pitch is that it should be executed from heart to heart. The quarterback is pitching the ball from his chest directly to the pitch man's chest. When the quarterback pitches the ball he should step towards the pitch man with the foot to the pitch side. This will allow him to see the ball be caught as well as close his hips to the defense which will serve to soften the blow. When major hits occur on a quarterback during the pitch phase of an option it is normally because the defender has gotten a clean hit on the quarterbacks chest.

With the creation of Run Pass Options many teams are adding a down field receiving threat to the mesh. One popular route that has been used is the dump route where a slot will get about 4-5 yards downfield and find a hole in the defensive zone and sits in the hole with his shoulder square to the QB. Another route that is becoming more popular is a post by the #1 WR and the Quarterback will read the Safety. While these get used often without a doubt the most popular route to combine to a mesh is the Bubble Route.

When reading a pass or run option the Quarterback should still be thinking "I am going to run this ball unless the defender can tackle me for less than four yards." Just like a pitch read the pass read can be difficult because the Quarterback is reading a defender in space. When deciding whether to throw the bubble route or not it's important that the QB is attacking downhill. Just like when he was deciding to pitch by attacking the overhang player going downhill the QB forces him to make a choice. One trick that helps the Quarterback is to pump fake a throw to the receiver. This is a very quick, safe way to freeze the defender which gives the QB space to get to four yards. From the Quarterback's perspective it's important that when he does decide to throw the ball he condenses his throw and really gets the ball out quickly.

Teaching the Plays

When teaching specific plays to the QB it's important to adapt the play so that it highlights the player's strengths and fits within your system. For this section we will focus on the majority of option plays that include a QB and Dive Back Mesh. Obviously every team runs plays in their own way. This section is not designed to dive into the blocking schemes but there is a quick drawing of what the scheme looks like. The purpose of these drawings is to make sure to communicate the play to the reader. There are many different ways to block the schemes so look at them as more of a general guide than a definitive blocking scheme.

Each play is broken down into three main stages. The first stage is the Footwork. This is path the QB must travel to arrive at his Pre-Mesh Position. It is vital during this stage that the QB moves quickly and efficiently to get into his Pre-Mesh position so he has a longer time to read the Dive Key.

The second phase that is unique to each play is the Read section. For this we will look at not only who the QB is reading but how he is reading that player. The QB will read the Dive Key on Midline much differently than the Dive Key on a Zone Read play. The final section is the Adjustments sections. Here we will look at some of the major different ways teams are running the scheme and how this changes the QB's footwork and reads.

As stated earlier, each team must adapt plays to meet their players strengths. These are the techniques for running these plays that have been successful, it's not the only way to run them but it provides a foundation to install the play and begin teaching it.

Midline

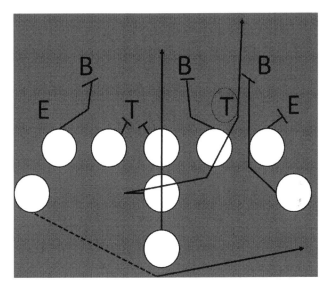

Midline vs. a 4-3 Defense

The Midline play is one of the staples of the flexbone option. It makes for a good play to teach because there is only one read and the play hits so quickly it makes it a read. While there are many ways to run the Midline play the general concept is that offense leaves the first defender past the center unblocked, this will be the read man. A running back will be running a path directly through the center, if the read man goes to tackle the running back the quarterback will pull the ball. If the read man ignores the running back and attempts to tackle the quarterback the ball will be handed off to the running back.

After the initial read there are a few ways to run the Midline play, either as a double option or a triple option. The difference is on a double option the quarterback will replace the defender in the B gap while in the triple option he will read the defensive end and either pitch or keep depending on his actions.

Midline: Under Center Footwork

The Midline is one of the quickest hitting plays in football. Because the play hits so quickly it puts a premium on footwork. With the speed of the Midline play there is no time for a quarterback to make a mistake with his footwork and recover, it has to be perfect from the first step to the last one.

There are multiple ways to teach the steps for the midline but the bottom line is that the quarterback must get his feet parallel to the running backs path which is straight through the center's feet. The main two ways of describing the quarterback's foot placement are by using the clock method or the quadrant method. If you are using the clock method the quarterback's first step is with his backside foot and will go backward to about 11 o'clock, his second step will be with his playside foot at around 7 o'clock. If you are using the quadrant method the quarterback's first step (again backside foot) is to quadrant 4 and his second step (playside foot) is to quadrant 3.

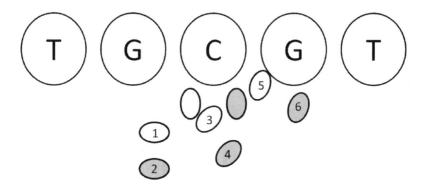

Midline footwork for Under Center

There are two ways that a quarterback can execute these steps. Beginners, in general, do better with the step method but some quarterbacks work best by using the hop method. The difference between the two is the amount of movements. With the step method there are two separate steps, the first step is a bucket step with the backside foot into quadrant 4 then he steps with the playside foot into quadrant 3. The hop method is going to combine these two and the quarterback will hop to his pre-mesh position directly from the snap.

Midline: Quarterback Reads

The number one thing to consider when coaching the read on Midline is the speed of the play. The speed of the play drives all of the quarterbacks thoughts when making his read. Because the plays hits so quick the quarterback wants to read the initial movement of the read man. If the QB waits for the reaction or deliberate movement of the read it will be too late. If the read key doesn't go directly for the RB at the snap of the ball he will not be able to make the tackle on the RB.

Many times the pre-snap alignment of the read key can be a huge indicator. As a general rule if the read key is past the B gap he will not be able to come in and make the tackle. The QB should still be making a read but the only way he would pull the ball would be if the read key screamed down into the A gap, which should be an easy read. On the other hand if there is a defender in the A gap the QB should again be thinking that he will probably be keeping the ball. As a general rule it is best to run Midline to an empty A gap.

If the play is run into an A gap defender (double A gaps or late stem) the QB is going to change his thought process. Previously the QB is planning on giving the ball unless the read key made a drastic move towards the RB. In the event of an occupied A Gap the QB is going to plan on keeping the ball unless the read key makes a dramatic move to defend the QB.

Midline: Variations-Mid Triple

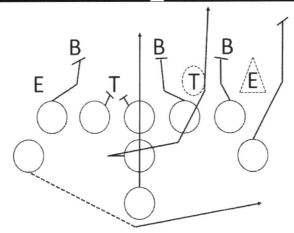

Midline Triple Option vs. 4-3 Defense

One of the constraints of the Midline play is to add a third option by reading the next defender outside of the dive read key, normally this will be the defensive end. Many times this play will be called because both the defensive tackle (dive read key) and the defensive end are crashing down. When this defensive stunt is run against the Midline as a double option it can be difficult for the PST to keep the DE out.

By calling Midline Triple the PST can let the Defensive End go and move onto a linebacker. The reason all of this matters to the QB is that means the Defensive End will more than likely be coming down to take the QB. If the QB is not ready to have a defender in his face right away this can result in a fumble or bad pitch. It is important that the QB thinks worst case scenario first and is prepared to pitch off the defensive end.

Midline: Variations- Shotgun/Showgun

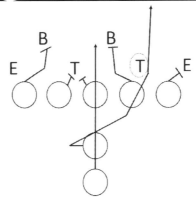

The Midline from the Showgun Formation

The Shotgun or Showgun version of Midline is largely the same but with a few subtle changes. The footwork will remain the same with the QB getting his feet parallel to the RB's path for the mesh. The difference is in the speed of the read. By removing the QB from Under Center the play has become a slower hitting play, obviously there are benefits as well, but when running the Midline the major concern is the speed of the read.

Because the play is hitting slower the read is now a slower read where the QB is forced to read the intention of the read key as opposed to his initial movement. This makes it a tougher read but it is a play that can still be very effective.

Teams are using the Midline play combined with Outside Zone as a way to slow down Defensive Tackles and make them easier to read. Here teams will normally run a play such as Outside Zone with the RB and leave the DT unblocked for the QB to read. This can really slow down a disruptive DT. Here it's important that the QB is again thinking I will hand the ball off unless the DT chases because the QB wants to avoid running head on into a DT. There is more on this in the Outside Zone section.

Inside Veer

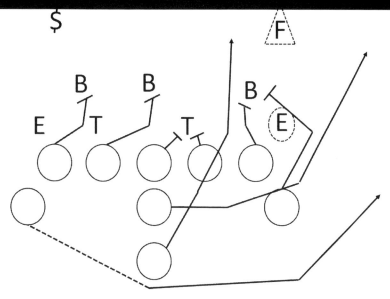

Inside Veer vs. a 4-3 Defense

The Inside Veer is the staple of the flexbone offense and, when mastered, can serve to be a whole offense within itself. There are quite a few moving parts to the Inside Veer and many different ways to block it. This makes it is a very expensive play to install. That being said there is a huge payoff if a team is able to master it. The general premise is that there will be a running back running somewhere inside the B gap (there are many opinions with where the running backs path should be, each with its own positives and negatives), a Quarterback who will be attacking through the C gap to the option alley and a pitch man who will be attacking the D gap to get to the option alley.

Inside Veer: Footwork

When teaching the quarterback the correct footwork both the quadrant and clock method can do the job. According to the clock method the quarterback's first step would be with his playside foot at about 4 o'clock. He would then step with his backside foot at around 2 o'clock. The quadrant method fits better with teaching the Inside Veer because the mesh can vary a little more than the footwork in Midline. In the quadrant method the quarterback would step with his playside foot into Quadrant II and his backside foot into quadrant I. One important point is that the toes should be parallel to the dive back's running path. Because the dive back is not running in a straight line this means that the quarterback's toes will not be parallel with the side line but have the backside foot slightly ahead of the playside foot.

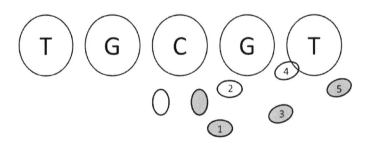

QB Footwork for Inside Veer from Under Center

Both the step and the hop method can be used effectively for Inside Veer. One dangerous part of the hop method is that the QB must make sure to get himself out far enough. If he does not gain enough ground on his hop the dive back will end up getting caught up on the PSG.

Regardless of how the footwork is taught it's crucial that the quarterback be in a great pre-mesh position with the ball extended back, knees bent and eyes on his read. While it's important the quarterback ends up at roughly the same position every play it's not that important how he gets there so resist the urge to over coach it. Coaching focus will have a much higher rate of return if it is focus on the reads the QB will be forced to make in order for the play to be successful.

Inside Veer: Reads

The triple option require two reads in a very quick secession, this causes it to be one of the hardest plays in football. In order to run the triple option effectively the quarterback can't be thinking during the play, he must instead rely on the instincts that have been developed through countless reps in practice. These instincts can be enhanced when the quarterback uses pre snap cues to help give him a more clear picture of what will happen after the snap.

In the Inside Veer scheme the quarterback will be reading the first player outside of the B gap. This is further away from the center which means that the play will be slightly slower hitting than the midline play. As a result the read will be a little longer. While on the midline play the quarterback wants to read the initial movement of the read key, on Inside Veer the QB will instead read the intention of the read key. The Inside Veer hits with enough of a delay that the read key can make an initial move away from the dive back and then come back to him or towards the dive key and then off to the QB. As a result the QB must use a full ride in his mesh and have a long read of the dive key. If the QB has a long ride he will have time to fully read the defender which will make his job much easier.

Inside Veer: Pitch Read

After coming off the mesh it's crucial that the QB gets downhill immediately and attacks down the field. If the QB bows back it gives the play side linebacker time to play both the dive and the QB. Once the QB detaches from the mesh he must immediately get his eyes to the pitch key and be ready for a blood stunt in which case he would pull and pitch quickly. This is something that must be practiced so the QB's instincts allow him to get the ball out without thinking. If the QB does not get a blood stunt he will attack the pitch key's inside hip and is thinking "I will run the ball unless the pitch key can tackle me for less than a 4 yard gain."

If the QB does get a pitch read he will deliver a pitch that is catchable and allows the pitch man to accelerate. If the QB's pitch forces the pitch back to slow down there is a chance the pitch key could play both the QB and pitch back. This takes away the advantage of the triple option.

If the QB gets a player who is feathering (stringing the play out) the QB can give a pitch fake, plant off his pitchside foot, and accelerate up field. One important point for the QB is that if he does get a keep read he gets up field immediately. Some coaches teach the QB and pitch man to keep the pitch option alive downfield. This is a very high risk play but can lead to a huge gain for the offense.

Inside Veer: Variations-Shotgun

Many teams like the Spread Shotgun Inside Veer because it allows them to spread the defense and get into their passing game easier while not changing anything, in terms of responsibilities, for the individual players. While the pitch back will need to take a longer motion the majority of the actual assignments stay the same.

When running the Inside Veer from the Shotgun it's important that the RB aligns a yard behind the QB. This allows for a longer mesh between the RB and QB. From the QBs perspective the major difference with the Inside Veer from the Shotgun will be his initial step. Instead of stepping into quadrant 3 or at 4-5 o'clock he will now be stepping up to quadrant 1 or 2 o'clock. His second step will take his backside foot parallel to the running backs mesh points. By stepping into the line he creates a longer read and gives the play time to develop.

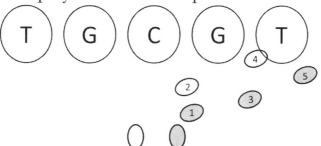

Footwork for Inside Veer from Shotgun

Inside Veer: Variations-Tags

There are many tags within the Inside Veer play including tags that will make the play a double option (taking away one of the option). It's impossible to go through every tag available to an offense running the Inside Veer but the major point is to make sure the quarterback is getting his eyes on the read immediately.

Outside Veer

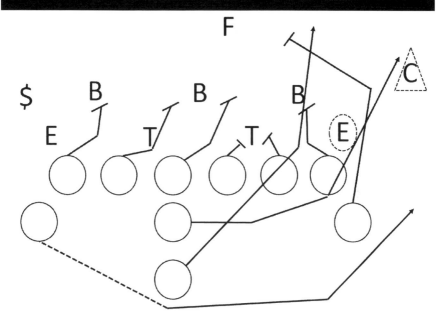

Outside Veer vs. 4-3 Defense

The outside veer is a very dangerous play that does not get as much use as it previously has. Outside Veer is designed to attack the C gap and is a very effective play to cause defenders to second guess their roles and responsibilities. Against an even front defense (above) the offense is reading the strong defensive end as the dive key and the cornerback as the pitch key. This means that the ball can get to the edge very quickly. Even if the QB gives the ball the dive back should have easy access to the option alley.

The difficulty with the Outside Veer is that it requires a 3 man surface. This means a Tight End or Unbalanced Tackle needs to be attached to the line. The other downside is that, from a QB perspective, he must really stretch to get the ball to mesh point.

Outside Veer: Footwork

For the outside veer the mesh point is by the C gap. This means that the QB will really need to push himself to get out to meet the dive back at the mesh. He does this by taking one large step with his playside foot and a quick hop off of his backside foot. After the hop from his backside foot he will land in a pre-mesh position with his feet parallel to the dive back's path.

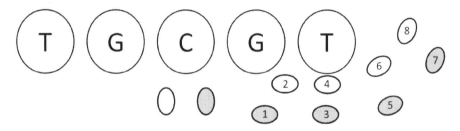

Footwork for Outside Veer from Under Center

The outside veer has the dive back aiming for just inside of the PST's outside leg. In order to run Outside Veer the offense must have a three man surface to the playside. This means that there must be a third player to block down on anyone in the C gap. If the C gap is unoccupied he will veer release to LB level. This could be a tight end, a tackle over or a wing back. What this means for the QB's read is that it will be even further removed from the center than Inside Veer. This means that the defender will have more time to decide who he will attack.

Outside Veer: Reads

Many times the QB will be reading a player who is not used to being read. This can result in the player doing a variety of different things. Normally the dive key will take a step forward, expecting to be responsible for the QB on Inside Veer. When he finds he is unblocked and sees the dive back coming at him normally he will go to take the dive back. It's important that the quarterback knows that the read will be a late read so he will be reading the dive key's secondary movement.

Due to the wider mesh point of the Outside Veer it's even more important that the QB attack directly downhill. A lot of times on the Outside Veer play the Quarterback is reading the overhang player. When this overhang player commits to the dive back the QB now has free access to the option alley. Reading an overhang player is much different than reading a Defensive Tackle or End. The players who tend to play in the overhang role (OLB or SS) are more comfortable playing in space and are much better at changing direction. This makes it crucial for the QB to have a long mesh and not make a choice until the defender has totally committed to stopping the dive back or the quarterback.

While it is harder to read the overhang player, by reading him the QB normally is able to break contain and get to the edge very quickly. Once the QB makes his read he is attacking the Safety or Cornerback as the pitch read. This means that the pitch read will be further down field. As a result the Outside Veer can be very stressful on the pitch portion of the play. The pitch player must do an excellent job staying in a pitch relationship down the field.

Inside Zone

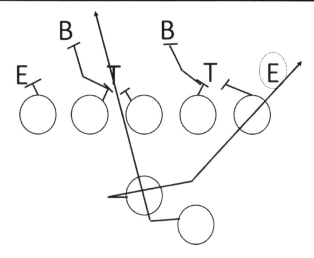

Inside Zone vs. 4-2 Defense
NB. I removed a box player because Inside Zone Read is normally from a formation that forces the defense to have a 6 man box

The Inside Zone is a play that has been sweeping across football due to it's versatility and the ability to use it to read a variety of different defenders. By using the Inside Zone from the shotgun teams have been able to read defensive linemen, linebackers and defensive backs. This book will not get into the schemes of who to read but instead will focus on the universal mechanics of the read. These mechanics will stay the same regardless of who the QB is reading.

Inside Zone: Footwork

While there are many ways to teach the Inside Zone play the one common denominator is that it is designed to run inside. The quarterback can use his footwork to help the running back keep the ball inside. When the quarterback receives the snap he is looking to get his feet parallel to the running back's path. To do this he will take a bucket step with his backside foot and then square up to the RB's path by bringing his front side foot parallel. From here he will get into a great pre-mesh position and get his eyes on his read key. Just like the Midline, some QBs do better using the hop technique so it's important to teach that as an option as well.

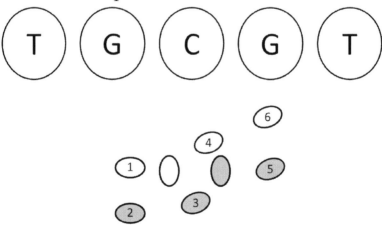

Footwork for Inside Zone Read from Shotgun
NB. This would be Inside Zone Left

Inside Zone: Reads

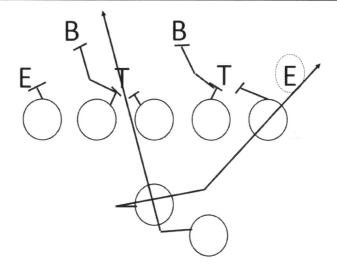

Inside Zone vs. 4-2 Defense
NB. I removed a box player because Inside Zone Read is
normally from a formation that forces the defense to have a 6
man box

The best part of the Inside Zone is the ability to vary who the quarterback is reading. Many times the Quarterback will be reading the backside defensive end but with the creation of RPOs teams have been reading players at the first second or even the third level. Regardless of which player the quarterback is reading the principles remain the same. He should have a great pre-mesh position with the ball reached back and his eyes on his read. It is critical that the QB have a long mesh so he can read the reaction of the read key.

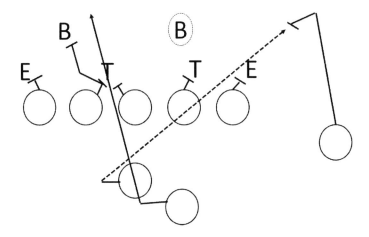

A different version of Zone Read with the QB reading the BSLB

Outside Zone

The Outside Zone play is another play that is growing in popularity due to who the Quarterback can read. While many teams continue to read the backside defensive end some teams have moved into reading a PS Interior lineman while others have started to reading the force player (normally the OLB or Safety). Regardless of who the Quarterback is reading, his footwork and mesh mechanics will remain the same.

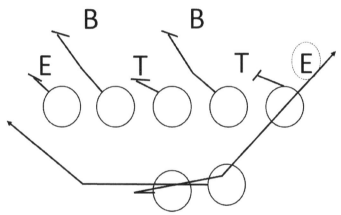

Outside Zone vs. 4-2 Defense
NB. I removed a box player because Outside Zone Read is normally from a formation that forces the defense to have a 6 man box

Outside Zone: Footwork

The footwork of the Quarterback can vary slightly depending on who is running the ball. In the event that the play is being run by a RB coming across his face the quarterback will take two steps directly backwards. This will leave his shoulders parallel to the running backs path and allow the Running Back a clean path to the edge.

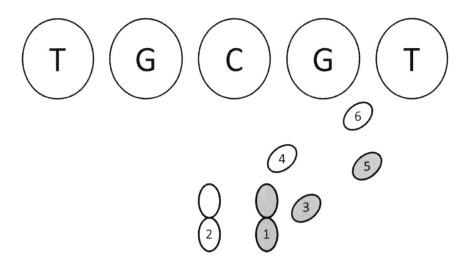

QB's footwork on Outside Zone to a RB
NB This would be Outside Zone Left

If the Outside Zone is being run by a player who is going in motion (Jet Sweep) the quarterback will take the snap and remain stationary. It's important he remains stationary so the motion man can have a guaranteed target to go to since he is moving quickly and is still responsible for the mesh.

Outside Zone: Reads

In the Outside Zone the quarterback is still thinking that he will be giving the ball unless the read key can make the tackle for less than 4 yards. When it is a backfield player running the Outside Zone (man not coming in motion) the mesh will be a full mesh so the QB can read the intentions of his key. If the man running the ball is a motion man it will be a very quick mesh since the motion man should be accelerating through the ball. This makes it critical that the QB has his eyes on the read man and is thinking give unless.

Some teams will use Outside Zone to control a dominant Defensive Tackle by reading the tackle instead of block him. This combines the Midline and Outside Zone and creates a very difficult play to defend. It's important that the QB is always thinking give the ball so he does not run head first into a defensive tackle. The QB also must do a good job of replacing that DT and getting up field quickly.

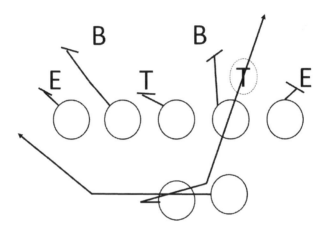

Outside Zone Reading the DT vs. 4-2 Defense
NB. I removed a box player because Outside Zone Read is normally from a formation that forces the defense to have a 6 man box

Inverted Power

The Inverted Power Read has swept across the football landscape. It is a great play to feature a bigger bruising runner at QB and quicker player at RB. One of the first people to really popularize this was Cam Newton at Auburn or Tim Tebow at Florida. This play can also be a great change up to get the RB with the ball on the outside or get the QB some carries if the defense is intentionally taking either one away in the option game.

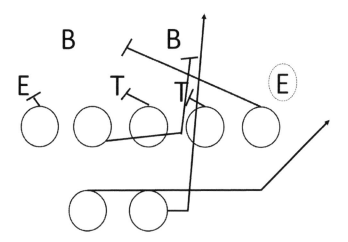

Inverted Power vs. 4-2 Defense
NB. I removed a box player because Inverted Power is normally from a formation that forces the defense to have a 6 man box

This play will have the line blocking a standard Power play but not kicking out the C Gap player. Instead the QB will be reading him. By using the Power blocking scheme the offense gains a two man advantage in the box. They gain one man by reading a player instead of blocking him. The offense gains a second player when it pulls the backside Guard. This advantage allows the offense to attack the perimeter where it now has a numbers advantage with the RB running the Sweep play or the interior where the QB and pulling Guard give them an advantage.

Inverted Power: Footwork

The Inverted Power Read can be a difficult play to read but is much tougher for the defense to stop. For this play the QB will be combining his Outside Zone footwork with a playside read. The crucial teaching point here is to make sure the QB keeps his path tight to the gapping unit and does not bend his path outside the B Gap. By keeping his path tight he forces the Dive Key to make a choice and stops him from playing both the RB and the QB.

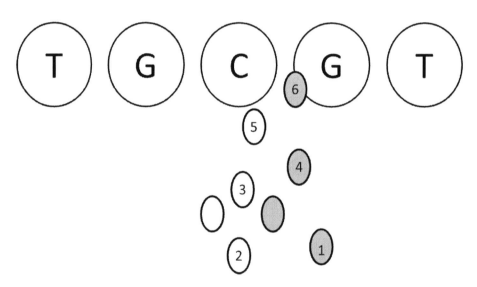

Inverted Power Footwork

This play has become associated with shuffling laterally from the QB during the mesh. While this is an effective technique for stretching the mesh out it brings the QB wider which makes the read harder. When teaching this play it is best to tell the QB, at least when installing the play, to not shuffle on the play. He will naturally move laterally a little bit but he must fight the urge to shuffle too wide. Instead as the Dive Back comes across his face he should transfer all of his weight to his playside foot. When the Dive Back clears his face he will step first with his backside foot directly downhill. This will allow him to accelerate from the mesh and keep his running path tight to the gapping unit.

Inverted Power: Reads

The read process for the Inverted Power is a little different. The RB is now running the wider play (in a Zone scheme he's running Outside Zone) while the QB is running the portion of the play that is hitting between the tackles (Power). When reading the Defensive End the QB is still going to be thinking that he will give the ball unless that Defensive End can tackle the RB. The reason behind this is that the RB will be running with momentum while the QB will need to transfer his momentum from moving sideways to moving forward. As a result the RB will be much more likely to break any arm tackles.

It's important that the QB has a long read so that he is able read the intentions of the Dive Key. The Inverted Read is an even longer read than an Outside Veer read, because of this the Read Key has a long time to choose how he is going to play the key and has time to bluff. This makes it crucial that the QB reads the intentions of the Dive Key. Early in the game he may have a few wrong reads, this is part of the reason it's so important that if there is any doubt he gives the ball. Normally the RB is much better equipped to deal with a hit from a Defensive End than the QB.

Conclusion

In conclusion teaching the mesh, like teaching any complex skill, is about breaking down the process into essential factors. Once the skill has been broken down into smaller, manageable pieces it is much easier for the player to know what he should be focusing on. These smaller sections also help the Coach focus on one or two key things. This allows both the player and coach to be on the same page in each drill which increases productivity.

When applying this system for teaching the mesh it's important to remember that the goal of any play is to put the player in the best possible position for him to be successful. When the Coach is consistently able to put his players in positions to be successful he creates an environment where that player can show their natural talents and benefit the team.

Good luck this season. I hope you were able to get something to improve yourself and your players from this EBook. Feel free to contact me thru email DWeitz7@gmail.com or Twitter @DWeitz7 if you have any questions.

Coach Weitz

46621719R00035

Made in the USA
Middletown, DE
04 August 2017